by the same author

poetry
TONIGHT'S LOVER (limited edition)
A VIOLENT COUNTRY
AFTER DARK
TRUCE (limited edition)
DREAMS OF THE DEAD
MISTER PUNCH
STORYBOOK HERO (limited edition)
NEWS FROM THE FRONT
THE POTTED PRIEST (limited edition)
A BIRD'S IDEA OF FLIGHT
MARRIAGE
LEGION
SELECTED POEMS 1969–2005

THE SORROW OF SARAJEVO (limited edition)
(English versions of poems by Goran Simić)
SPRINTING FROM THE GRAVEYARD
(English versions of poems by Goran Simić)

as editor
SAVREMENA BRITANSKA POEZIJA
(for the Writers' Union, Sarajevo; with Mario Suško)
RAISING THE IRON
(for the Palace Theatre, Watford)
ANOTHER ROUND AT THE PILLARS: A FESTSCHRIFT FOR IAN HAMILTON

words for music
SERENADE THE SILKIE (music by Julian Grant)
WHEN SHE DIED (music by Jonathan Dove)
CRIME FICTION (music by Huw Watkins)
GAWAIN (music by Harrison Birtwistle)
THE WOMAN AND THE HARE (music by Harrison Birtwistle)
THE RING DANCE OF THE NAZARENE (music by Harrison Birtwistle)
THE MINOTAUR (music by Harrison Birtwistle)
THE CORRIDOR (music by Harrison Birtwistle)

fiction
FROM AN INLAND SEA

NIGHT

DAVID HARSENT

Night

ff

faber and faber

First published in 2011
by Faber and Faber Ltd
Bloomsbury House
74–77 Great Russell Street
London WC1B 3DA

Typeset by Faber and Faber Ltd
Printed in England by T. J. International Ltd, Padstow, Cornwall

A CIP record for this book
is available from the British Library

ISBN 978–0–571–25563–4

2 4 6 8 10 9 7 5 3

To Jo Shapcott

The Bitch Supreme in spangles and tulle, Old Bloody Bones,
The Beggar King and Sheela-na-Gig – all out on the town.
They're up for Happy Hour which lasts from dusk to dawn.

Night in the City of Locks casts a shadow across the moon.
Lights come on in the Bounty House and the Palace of Porn.
There's no way of telling blind from sighted, diehard from drone.

The serial offenders square up to the gladsome insane.
The milksop twins (it's come to this) face each other down.
The lipless child in the corner weeps tears of stone.

In the tenement cul-de-sacs the chancers cut and run.
Something fronts in the dark that could be shadow or stain.
There's a smell of scorch in the air. And the time to be gone has gone.

Acknowledgements

Thanks are due to the editors of the following journals, publications and organizations who first published or commissioned some of the poems in this book: *Blinking Eye*, *Brick* (Canada), *London Review of Books*, *New Yorker*, *Poem for Today* (BBC Radio 3), *Poetry* (USA), *Poetry London*, *Poetry Review*, *Spectator*, *Times Literary Supplement*, *Warwick Review*.

'The Hut in Question' was commissioned for *Branch Lines: Edward Thomas and Contemporary Poetry*, edited by Guy Cuthbertson and Lucy Newlyn (Enitharmon).

'Spatchcock' was commissioned for *Tate Etc.* at The Tate Gallery Website. The painting I had in mind was Jean Dubuffet's *L'Arbre de fluides*. The last line is drawn from Susan Hiller's notes to her installation *From the Freud Museum*. Both works can be found in Tate Modern.

'The Death of Cain' was commissioned by Magma.

The five 'Blood' poems were commissioned by *The Verb* (BBC Radio 3). Blood alley is the name given to a large marble, clear glass except for the twist of red at its heart. A Bloodvein is a moth whose pale cream colouring is broken only by a thin line of red that goes from wing-tip to wing-tip.

'Suburb' was commissioned by The Royal Philharmonic Society.

'The Queen Bee Canticles' were commissioned by Poet in the City, supported by the City of London Festival and Gresham College.

'Vanitas' appeared in *A Century of Poetry Review*, edited by Fiona Sampson (Carcanet). The poem has been set to music by Harrison Birtwistle.

Contents

NIGHT

Rota Fortunae

Dawn darkness is a bare blue light
and there's a sound coming at you, most likely brought on the wind
from a hillside forest or nicked off the skim of the sea . . .

So you're humming that long, slow note as you broach the day,
and the dogs of dawn are all one voice as you step
down from your home sweet home, your *tour-de-folie*,

and before you get the other side of the gate
comes a smash and clatter of wings as a thing takes flight
from a point just above your head and has you pinned

by joy-in-fear as its lift-off shakes from the Tree
of Love and Forgetting something much like a fruit
that sits, just so, in the cup of your hand,

though it would take a bigger fool than you to bite
into that honeyed rump, as if you hadn't sinned
enough, as if you wouldn't have to pay

your share for each day of solitude, each night
when your dreams of flight and falling left you stunned.
God help the merely fortunate: lives lived in shades of grey –

let's leave them to contentment . . . yes . . . and let's agree
luck is a different darling; luck, in fact, is what
the Daughters of Necessity have planned

for you, this way or that: the turn of a key,
or else the turn of a card, that might
bring you from dawn shadow into the light of day

on a morning like this and set you in the way
of that seascape blown raw, that hillside, that self-same note,
the drone still in your ear, though somewhat dimmed,

and no way to know what's next, what sleight
of hand those hags might bring to the game, or why
it's you at all, or whether the black and white,

the yin and yang, that ever-turning wheel, its rote:
I rise, I rule, I fall, and *I am crushed,*
will play out in your favour. See where the doomed and damned

look up to the sky as it trembles and tears, each lashed
to a spar or spoke: going under, or all but gone; and see where the rest
lift their hands to heaven, out of sight

except to those beside them and above, the newly blessed
who imagine they've found their rightful place in the
    turn-and-turn-about,
though the sudden sun on their faces, the cool, clean air will cost

all that they have and more, since that lofty inch-by-inch
is simply the way of death, is death
as shiftless shadow, death as that hint in the air, as the first

waking thought, death as a face in the street,
a face in a photo-album long since lost,
is death the dreamer, death the locksmith, death now cast

as a friend in need, death as the thin
end of the wedge, is the *fuddle* of death, the way death sidles in
with a nod and a cough, is death self-styled,

is the niff, the nub, the rub of death, is death at a pinch,
death in a poke, death as a bastard child,
and that note you sang was the voices of those on the wheel

teased out to a single sound that might have chilled
the blood of a man less troubled; and all the while
they were singing it back to you, or singing it back to the wind;

so the dogs, the fallen fruit, the wash of air that belled
and thrummed as the creature broke from the tree, the blind
luck that brought you this far – all are part of a deal

struck at the hour of your birth, part of a plan that always held
this very moment, when you pause to think
of the dream that had you stalled somehow above a depthless blank

of sky and sea . . . and there floods in, now as never before, that sense
of giving yourself over to chance
that will turn you for home, or take you to the brink.

Ghosts

They bring with them a coldness, as tradition demands,
and a light, dry odour of rot
much like worm in wood, and bring a chorus of cries

to fill the air as if it were birdsong, and bring in their open hands
tokens of themselves, a letter, a snapshot,
and bring some trace of their point of departure, a smudge

on the shoe, a stain on the sleeve, and bring the disguise
they lived under, stitched with their names,
hoping you'll give them the nod, hoping you'll recognise

something, perhaps, of the old times, the fun and games,
while they shuffle up as if they stood on the edge
of night so a nudge would tip them over, and bring

a dew of death that settles on picture-frames,
on pelmets, on clothes in the closet, on books,
on your eyelash, to make a prism through which you get

a broken image of what must be a stage-set
of the Peaceable Kingdom – a front
for that place you only ever find in dreams,

its undrinkable rivers, its scrubland of snarls and hooks,
horizons gone askew,
beasts hamstrung and walking on their hocks,

and bring their long-lost hopes which they lay at your feet
then stand back, stand apart,
hairless, soft-skinned, their eyes bright blue

like the eyes of the newborn, and bearing a look
of matchless sorrow as would, for sure,
stop the heart of whoever it is they take you for.

The Garden in Fading Light

Here is your key. It was specially cut. If the door
to the garden blows shut as you enter, at least
you'll have your own key, though the way out is not

really the same. That smell is just what you take it to be:
loosestrife and dogwood and rot, though be sure
that whatever you cut will keep, whatever you lost

will somehow come to light, which is, of course, the last
thing you want. There are those who come here to be
beside themselves, others with eyes tight shut; you might

prefer not to think of that, and you might prefer
to steer clear of the hut at the garden's end, though more
seem drawn to it, the litter, the rat-run under the floor,

the bat in the rafters; perhaps they forget that night
falls more readily in gardens, and forget
the face in the water-butt, the addled egg in the nest,

and wander across that bare plot, six-by-four,
without feeling a thing. Call them ill-favoured, ill-met . . .
If you're here to settle a debt, as you seem to be,

you might want to call it quits, might think it best
to cut and run, what with the shadow-play in trees,
the note of panic evening brings to birdsong.

You'll find a way out soon enough; each wrong
turn will set you straight, and though you recognise
nothing at all and the light is fading fast,

the door will seem right enough and the key will fit
no doubt, as you open up, as you step across
to that troubling cut of moonshine in the street.

A View of the House from the Back of the Garden

In darkness. In rain. Yourself at the very point
where what's yours bleeds off through the palings
to *terra incognita*, and the night's blood-hunt
starts up in the brush: the notion of something smiling
as it slinks in now for the rush and sudden shunt.

A women is laying a table; the cloth
billows as it settles; a wine-glass catches the light.
A basket for bread, spoons and bowls for broth
as you know, just as you know how slight
a hold you have on this: a lit window, the faint
odour of iodine in the rainfall's push and pull.

Now she looks out, but you're invisible
as you planned, though maybe it's a failing
to stand at one remove, to watch, to want
everything stalled and held on an indrawn breath.

The house, the woman, the window, the lamplight falling
short of everything except bare earth –
can you see how it seems, can you tell
why you happen to be just here, where the garden path
runs off to black, still watching
as she turns away, sharply, as if in fright,
while the downpour thickens and her shadow on the wall,
trembling, is given over to the night?

Surely it's that moment from the myth
in which you look back and everything goes to hell.

The Garden in Sunlight

Go by white poppies, white tulips, white flags, go by
the white willow arch, go by the apple tree, its full white crop,

go by the pond where white-eyed fish
slide by deeper each day, then out to the lawn, its trackless white

a mirror image of the trackless sky;
but think now: after you've set foot you're on a wish

and a promise, adrift in white's slow creep
away and over the edge, though something takes you straight

to those little spoil-heaps: bone that breaks to ash
under your hand . . . and you backtrack, hoping for sight

of the house, perhaps, or the garden gate, or the street,
but it's white-on-white however hard you try,

and a hum in the air, white noise, which could be some rash
report of you: figment, divertimento, little white lie.

The Garden in Dream

I

There it is, the cicatrice of lichen
that tags clean air, and 'mountain lady's slipper',
so rare that everything else must slip and sicken.

II

Full-length on the lawn, sharing their copy of *Home
and Garden*, her hair brushing his wrist as he turns the page.
Call it love in a mist. Call it Stockholm syndrome.

III

Blood-cake rolled from the sack and dug well in.
Orchids at their stakes fatten on this:
their pucker-and-pout, their taint, their sense of sin.

IV

There, on the 'rustic bench': Dido, Eurydice, the girl
from the cash and carry. Don't worry at why or whether;
what brings them together is nothing more than guile.

V

Black cross-tracks in the dew from hedge
to house where something shambled through, then back
from house to hedge: whatever leaves a smudge.

VI

Small fires burn under bramble; imagine a plain
seen from a tower at night; they'll bring up
the trebuchets and ballistae at dawn.

VII

This flower's baby blue seems almost bland
except, when you hold it close, you get the true
depth; and when you look away, you're blind.

VIII

Children's shadows on the grass: it goes all day,
the right game in the wrong way; and every night
'Black-contra-Black' becomes their shadow-play.

IX

The garden's weather is frost over stone, is small
rain up from the west, is wind-backed snow,
is whatever you need, or else is nothing at all.

X

A bird on every bough. The whole place cluttered with sunlight.
Something half-heard as the last guest leaves.
Breakage. Spillage. Wreckage of tansy and eyebright.

The Garden Hammock

Your book is *Summer* by Edith Wharton. A smell
off the borders of something becoming inedible.
Between sleeping and waking, almost nothing at all.

There's music in this, there would have to be: a swell
of strings and bells becoming inaudible,
note by note, before you latch on to it. The girl

in the story won't prosper, that's easy enough to tell.
How did night come on like that? The sky is full
of birds, wingbeats in darkness becoming indelible.

The Long Walk to the End of the Garden

The rusty stain on the pillow, the rumble of pain
in your knee, impromptus of a dream in which

you hacked your way out again and again, the dawn
fading up from the green-blue-green of the silver birch,

a flourish on the surface of the pond, a ragged skein
of bindweed on the stone-cold statuette

of that thin-lipped girl from the dream, the odds-on bet
that nothing returns or renews, that the stain

is just what it seems, that the sudden catch
in the throat, the moment of blind regret,

will be all in all, that your way through the garden wet
will take you, for sure, out by the willow-arch

on a morning much like this, and into the lane
beyond which must lie the far field, beyond which

a nameless road, beyond which a landline drawn
in clumsy charcoal below a clumsy sketch

of yourself as pseudocide, a frantic silhouette
soon smudged to shadow by incoming rain.

The Garden Goddess

Out by the woodpile at three a.m., knock-kneed and shitfaced,
lost in your own backyard,
you pour a libation that comes straight from the dregs and she drinks it.

Or you stand at a sinkful of broken this and that
wide-eyed and with nary a hint of what's next,
as she goes by with her Tesco bags and a fifth of gin in her pocket.

She keeps unholy hours. There's a chance you'll see her naked
at noon among roses; a fair chance, too,
that in bending to cup a bloom, she'll show you the little widget

of her arsehole, damson-sweet and, some say, the very fount
of knowledge, though certain dream-
images, featuring sweats and the shakes, somehow cause me to doubt it.

Capricious? Of course. She'll as likely spit in your eye as lay
a calming hand on your cheek, although
it's known that she once gave up a bindweed and bottletop bracelet

that carried a certain charge, a link of some kind, a portal,
that could rush you all the way
to the back of the garden and open the gate and set your foot on the snicket

that leads to the ever-notorious 'place beyond', and the way
thorny and the light gone bad and the wind rising,
which is why you'd most likely decide to take her advice and forget it.

As she turns to favour you with that self-same rose, you might notice
how her shoulder-blades jut and curve
like the folded wings of an angel, how she smells very slightly of civet,

how her nose is off-true, as if she had once been the victim
of a random attack, how the dark of her eye
can bring you on, or the wet of her lip, how the dab of cuckoo-spit

[14]

that fell to her thigh from some dead-head or seed-pod
has left a trickle of glisten,
some time later described in your journal as 'slick, like a scar in velvet'.

As for why rain works round her, or how things green
when she moves among them, or what
music it is she brings with her, these things must remain, as always, her secret,

as must the true tale of the love of her life, who saw her
exactly as you see her now, and took
her kiss and changed, so we're told, in a moment from mortal to misfit.

Blood Relative

His footsteps in yours, the moment of waking that same
redeye view of the world, his dottle deep

in your lung, his kiss your gift to give: the sudden sharp
dip of his head, the bloodbead on a lover's lip,

his arrival in the room your moment of fame,
his easy laugh, his clever guess, his word to the wise the sum

of all you are, all you could ever be, and your other name,
given in passion, in trust, is nothing more than a slip

of the tongue, and no one but yourself to blame
for the hand-in-hand, the cheek-to-cheek, the side-by-side as you sleep.

Tourist Trap

The wall of skulls: ah, yes; eye-dimples outward, some holding a sip of rain.
The craftsmen worked just this side of the fracture-point in bone.
Something was said of it once, we're told, that must never be said again.

Ballad

As I walked by the riverside
Death came up to me
He said, 'This river runs, my friend,
To a deep and darkening sea

And what goes over at the weir
Can never come again
Whether it be sweet heartsease
Or whether it be pain

All the tears shed in the world
Will trickle to this flow
And what that weight of weeping tells
Only I can know

Watch how the river thickens now
And carries with the flood
Sweat from mines and factories
From battlefields the blood

Spittle from the prison yard
And from the graveyard, clay
And all the work of evil hands
That can't be washed away

The milt and meltings of the drowned
Caught up with butcher's spill
Turn with the tug of the morning tide
And leach to the midstream swill

Lightless boats unload their freight
Of malice and dismay
Bringing the bright and beautiful
To ruin in a day

All the stones are cold and blind
All the winds are ill
All the birds are silent
And all the fish are still

No one stands where you now stand
Without feeling the pull
The river brings to flesh and blood
When rolling at the full

So take a step and take a step
And take a step away
For you and I are set to meet
By here another day

When the water's at the flood and fierce
And colder than my hand
As I take you past the bankside trees
Out to the last of the land

And the running river tells a tale
Of the life you should have led
And the stars and moon are the first you see
Of the reachless riverbed.'

Blood Heat

Full length under a wide white sky in a place like this, or a place
you think you remember, or wherever it is she happens to turn her face

to the sun, eyes open a moment, then the flare and crush
of red behind the lids and you at her side to watch the sudden blush

that prickles her skin, the first fine hint of burn, as you get
the tip of your tongue to her cheek for the salt-lick of her sweat.

The Death of Cain

*Lamech, a descendant of Cain, goes hunting. A creature
covered in a black pelt breaks cover. Lamech lines up on it
and looses an arrow. The creature is mortally wounded. It is
Cain, who then laments his life as an outcast, but allows that
it was punishment for killing his brother. Intrigued, Lamech
asks Cain why he murdered Abel.*

Because he had a mouth on him like sulphur;
because he gave me no respect;
because I was ever brother and no other;
because he smiled even as he slept
(or so she said); because my heart
carries a weight of hatred that will never
lift nor leave me even when I'm dead.

Although in all the world I stand apart
and live within the shadow of my name,
God's curse on my head and on my head
the curses of my mother and my father,
although I lie here at your feet
speaking through blood and bile, I don't regret it;
each night I dream of even blacker fame,
then bad luck wakes me and I rise to greet it.

Lamech, I'm close enough to smell your sin.
I'll see you in hell where all the unforgiven,
the unforgiving, are sworn to come together
bare-headed under a murderous sun
or naked in never-ending winter weather.

from the Cornish of William Jordan, circa 1611

Live Theatre

The plot draws darkness down. The lover betrayed
betrays in turn. That 'slip of a girl' who showed
such promise must turn again to the heartless trade.

~

The Field of Repentance is astro-turf; the priest
calls on the Resurrection Man. The ghost
of the murderee in the attic is waiting to be released.

~

It's the Ice Queen's turn to get down in the gutter
with the Demon Lover. The alchemist's daughter
transcribes, all night, from the soft morse of his stutter.

~

The women of the house are lost in song; their sorrow
waits on them as it should. The sometime hero
has alibis for tomorrow and tomorrow.

~

The happy couple are hollow-eyed with love; their flight
into joy is hazardous. The man in the seersucker suit
denies he was anywhere near the place that night.

~

There's nothing left of the girl on the swing but a sigh
and a gesture crumpling the air. A silkie steps from the sea
stranded between the wherefore and the why.

~

One in a state of grace, one peevish: the lip-synch twins
break out the psilocybin. The prodigal returns
to the amped-up pre-record of a thousand violins.

∼

They truck the death-bed in; the Avenging Angel stands
in line, tight-lipped, bright-eyed. The leading man's
in the seat next to yours, worn out, his head in his hands.

The Duffel Bag

God's blood beads on the tarmac and something rough is boiling up
just this side of the vanishing-point, so it's probably time to get

off this stretch of blacktop and into the wayside bar, where every cup
runneth over and you breast a thickening fret

of stogie-smoke to get to the dank back room where a high stakes game
turns against you despite your trey of jacks, and soon enough

you're in way over your head with nothing and no one to blame
but the luck you've been getting since first you threw your stuff

into a duffel-bag and hooked up with the halt and lame,
with the grifters and drifters, the diehards, the masters of bluff,

the very bastards, in fact, who are lifting the last of your stash.
So it's into the crapper and out through the window – you're free

to do whatever you must, so long as that purple-and-yellow blush
in the sky doesn't mean what it seems, so long as that lick of flame

from the hard-shoulder spillage doesn't travel as far as the scree
of garbage in the lay-by, so long as that's not your name

in the red-top front-page splash on the trailer-trash kidnappee.
Just keep to the shadow-side, keep in under the lee

of roadside billboards, bed down in the roadside scrub, your dream
of Ithaca, that ghost town, though the rest is mystery –

what brought you to this and who might take the blame,
and how to get from the open road to a sight of the open sea.

Moppet

Consider the rip for a mouth, the rip in the crotch, the hank of hair,
consider the flair for ill-fortune, the empty stare, the done deal
with sorrow, the rich and rare nest-egg of dreams, the share and share
alike in matters of loss, the payments in kind, the liking for blind
bets, for truth or dare; consider the threadbare get up, the make-up
beyond repair, the tin-tack teeth, consider the dungeon voice
wanting nothing more than bare house-room, and nothing less
than hand-in-glove, a pigeon pair given over to make and mend,
to touch and go, to wear and tear, and all it takes is this: forswear
flint and fire, stay silent, be white on white, live in dead air.

Vanitas

The death's-head bell has a tongue like a barber's strop
capped with a dangle of shot . . . meanwhile

she takes the flower she was bound to cut
and places it in the vase, displacing a single drop

of water onto the satin cloth, and stoops to set
a sand-clock on the other side. It's troubling to see the weal

that tracks from her cheek to her throat and out of sight
by the ruche of her blouse; the hang of her lower lip,

fattened by weeping; the way the light
brings a touch of blue to her cheekbone, the first of night.

The garden is crowding the window. From where I sit,
I can watch the silhouettes of nightbirds fall

on the upper panes, grow still a moment, then haul
off and away, as if they had rested briefly in the glaze;

but the woman, without asking, brings a light
the better to see herself in the darkening glass

her face amid a smudge of wings and trees
as she stands looking out but also looking back

to me in my chair, near-breathless as I can get,
silent, saying nothing with my eyes.

This is a lesson, I think, in how to feel:
the bloom, the woman, her wound, that the chair is set

slightly to one side, that my hands now fall
slack to my lap . . . and, of course, love in the guise

of a skull licked clean, the dome chock-full
of darkness, of errant music, of thoughts of me.

II

Imagine a shred of song drawn through a blown egg, think
of a whisper held in an empty house, of a promise made

in a moment of weakness, of who you have to thank
as the eye-sockets flicker and fill, as the lips repair,

the voice thin but distinct: *You see in me
the last of the feckless romancers: his smile, the smile*

*of the beside companion, the smile-in-air
of the trickster, the smile of betrayer betrayed,*

*of the just-abandoned or else the soon-to-be,
of the hangman, the hanged man, the dog-faced boy,*

*the hobbledehoy, the jack-in-the-box, the shill,
of tyrant and martyr coming together in joy.*

The woman starts the clock; a petal falls;
darkness settles to perfect night; the bell

carries a note too deep or else too shrill
to break the silence. Best to be watchful now, best to be still,

what happens next is anybody's guess:
the window a mirror perhaps, the room a wilderness.

Blood Alley

Your childhood token, a sickle of red in the glass, albino eye,
eye of the night-lamped hare; a perfect lob would break the circle . . .

Now hold it close to the light and every fibril
seems to shred, as heart-blood hangs in water, that same dark dye –

shade of the dress she wore when you had your first full taste
of the pulp of her lip and the spittle off her tongue, the cost

to you being more than you had to give, which is why
the circle must break again and the dream unpick and the child be lost.

Scene One: A Beach

I

And this is where I've got to, pitched up on some shoreline
like any piece of wreckage, like something
once adrift, now simply lost, no given purpose,
no way of knowing where from, where to, no sense of direction,
just this notion of distance covered, this notion of release,
at what might be nightfall, might be daybreak, but no sign
to tell me which, no help at hand, only the subtle traction
of a rising tide nudging me up and on as if the thing
to do is get clear, get going, as if somewhere yet unseen
but only a short way off might prove to be the place
I'd always had in mind, as if a voice still waiting
to be heard might give me a start, perhaps a word
to work with, and I might somehow conjure a face
from a cloud and that sudden vision tell me everything.

II

I can hear the breakers and a rush of wings,
that's all. I can get to my feet. I can take the first
full step. I can open my eyes. I can see how light is cast
under the fold of the wave and how it hangs
forward of the water when it falls. As for the rest,
there's only the blur and hum that always lies
at the near side of what comes next, or what is past.

III

Begin in silence, the sea drawn back
to a distant smudge beneath a fading moon.
Shingle first, then turf and soon the seamless black
of a road that rolls to the edge, then on to stolen ground.
Everything I once recognised as mine

is strange to me now, and that stupendous lack
is what gives me my pace, what helps me on
towards the unheard, the invisible, the rare,
subtle as tears in rainfall, as breath on the wind . . .
The road delivers me. The residue of prayer
lies on my lip like salt. The place is dust
in a bowl of barren hills. A voice declares
*Your starting point is grief; you must
get used to this.* To being out of mind; to being moonblind.

IV

Go from here, go from the shoreline again,
the sun just up, frost on the open ground, a blue
haze in the distance that must be the city's spew.
I'm at odds with myself; I shift, somehow, in my skin;
my bones are wrong; my eye-line's out of true . . .
What next? I'll follow the long thin line
of my shadow until I find somewhere to get to.

V

Now this house on the outskirts: its bald, blind look,
and a room in the house where someone sits
barely breathing, hands folded, eyes wide, and waits
for the sound of a voice, perhaps, or the sound of a lock
turning, someone whose view of the window gives back
only night-day-night; but here's my face at the glass
to observe the white walls, the bare floor, the seated figure,
to return that steady stare, to deliver like for like,
as if a question might be put, as if something might pass
between us that would give me the clue to the room,
to the left-over traces of night, shadows that gather

in corners, a silence that could split along its seam . . .
Time out of time; one reflection laid on the other.
I turn away as if I were turning from home.

VI

Rain off the sea, a sudden rush that smothers
the long line of the beach and turns it dark . . .
Rumble of stones in the undertow, dreck
scummed up at the tideline, oil and feathers,
the sky near-touchable, a rising wind at my back.
One horizon sliding towards me, and another
lost in blue however far I walk.

VII

Into the city grid, streets slammed down thus
by the Planner's iron hand which means you can go
only this way or that, and two by two
as intended, just like myself and whoever it is
walking beside me, silent, looking down
so as not to miss a step. There are houses with doors
but no windows, or sometimes it's windows
and no doors. Wherever they go they're in the zone
and seem to know it by the worried smiles, the eyes
closing for a moment as they pass. There are no trees
in the city square, or cafés, or fountains. Here they lean
on each other's arms, or hover in mid-stride
as, for a moment, do I, does he, until I step aside
knowing whoever he is he's better left alone.

VIII

Spindrift, skim of the sea torn off to fall just short
of where I'm knees-to-chin, arms wrapped about me, caught

in the lee of a breakwater, wondering how to get
the best out of this, how to tell the way back from the way
forward, if only by day, in good weather, if only by starlight.
The gulls are screaming, not weeping as people like to say.
There's nothing to hope for in this, and nothing to regret.

IX

A valley seen from a hillside, beyond which
a plain rolling out a chequerboard of rocks
and scrub beyond which a wood that quickly thins
to swamp beyond which a glint from tower blocks
beyond which a landscape showing no more than stitch
and patch from this distance through which runs
the only road, the road I've followed, it seems,
to the end and then beyond. In the valley, a river
of souls; on the plain, a sun-bleached cadaver;
in the wood, a gallows-branch; in the swamp a hand
reaching out; in the tower block a murder
that always goes unseen . . . and no surprise to find
a figure in that landscape, hammered by suns,
constantly going forward, constantly losing ground.

X

The ocean churns its junk of bones, its tar
and toxins, whatever might break
the surface of the menstruum, bald and white, whatever
beaches here, mongrel or throwback,
something just skin and finger, something just beak
and gill. All that rouses me now is fret and fever
and all that concerns me how deep, how dark, how far.

Bloodstain

Drench of the death-bed that drains to the floorboards and hangs
like a sweat of dew on the ceiling below . . . And where you found

that graceless image is for you alone to know, but it brings
with it a tang of salt, and a dry day by the sea then comes to mind:

raw sky and a cutting wind that left the man half-blind
from a scrap of something blown in from the other shore,

the tear of blood he caught up with his tongue, the nip of fear
you felt as he swivelled the white of his eye and you took

the mote on the tip of your finger, his shudder-sigh, his empty look
no different now to then, except for the dew of the sea on his cheek.

The Hut in Question

Rain, midnight rain, nothing but the wild rain
On this bleak hut, and solitude, and me
EDWARD THOMAS, 'Rain'

And here it is, slap on the co-ordinates,
nothing special of course,
a tar-paper roof (is it?) nailed to sloping slats,
a door that's flush to the floor, and grates
when you draw it back. Weather-worn, half-hidden by gorse
in full fire, it being that time of year; the window
thick with cobwebs, clarty candyfloss;
a hint of rot; things spongy underfoot.

Being here alone is easiest.
There are songbirds in the sedge
(I think it is) and a wind to clout the reeds, a test
of the place, as are these clouds: a long dark flow
pulling fast and heavy off the ridge . . .
Easiest given what we make of quest,
its self-regard, its fearsome lost-and-found, its need to know
the worst and wear its sorrows like a badge.

Do you get what I mean if I speak of light – half-light –
that seems to swarm: a mass
of particles folding and rolling as if you stood too close
to a screen when the image dies? The edge
of night . . . those forms that catch and hold
just at the brink where it's nearly but not quite.

I see, now, by that light. Rain finally coming in, the day
falling short, adrift in shades of grey,
and nowhere to get to from here, or so I guess,

with distances fading fast,
with the road I travelled by a thinning smudge,
with all that lay between us bagged and sold,
with voices in under the door that are nothing more nor less
than voices of those I loved, or said I did,
with nothing at all to mark
fear or fault, nothing to govern loss,
and limitless memory starting up in the dark.

Broken Glass

On one side of the mirror, me, myself, in doubt.
On the other, the man I mostly want to be.
See us clear as we turn and turn about.

～

I hold out my hand to the rain,
as if that 'simple act'
were something I might do again and again.

～

These are the saddest snaps I've ever seen.
My father in khaki. My father in khaki. My father
in khaki. Yes. My mother in bombazine.

～

Pi-dogs. A lemon sky. A Judas kiss.
A night in some shebeen. The view you get
from behind the gun. I dreamed all this.

～

A room hanging in silence. A sunstruck window.
Doors to left and right.
A sense of decorum tells you which way to go.

～

She kicked off her shoes. She unzipped and dropped her dress,
then stalled on a vacant look.
Next night the same, and the night after that, more or less.

～

Why not grub up a smidgen of turf from his grave?
Cultivate it. Trim it as you might
toenails or hair. Soon you'll know how to grieve.

~

A teardrop mask. White gloves. Crowds in the street.
She is running a fever; she's ill.
All the more reason, she thinks, to be indiscreet.

~

The ocean at night, where something tremendous leaps.
Did I say 'sleeps'?
Who knows what the darkness discovers?

~

A word unsaid, a withdrawal, a second guess
right at the wrong time . . .
The dry *clack-clack* of the abacus.

~

Waking, again, in tears for the moment lost
to the moment of waking;
all day long you walk with that same ghost.

~

The footfall of the uninvited guest.
The EntriCam.
Teeth and hair and pixilated lust.

~

The colour green, as if no other colour would do.
She was going through snow for sure,
so a long time back. So it might have been brown or blue.

~

A man steps off a tall building. Your task?
To remember the slinky undertone
of shoe-leather on brick; not much to ask.

~

Cock-crow. Clean linen. A sea-mist.
Tulips one side of a limestone wall.
Given time, I could complete this list.

~

This word from the edge of sleep: *abandonment.*
Oh, very clear since you ask.
And clearer still what it meant.

~

After all that, milady's final choice:
'Not bloodstone – *moon*stone.' And then:
'They say my true instrument is voice.'

~

A stipple of spit on the tiling. A snatch
of song. Machinery cranking up.
Rain-clouds as far as . . . Catnap. Mix and match.

~

She could touch you now, if she wanted. She could find
the little rub of blue where she touched you last,
not a bruise, exactly; not quite. She could do it blind.

~

'The ecstasy of animals,' you say, as if that pact
between pain and innocence
could return you to yourself intact.

~

At the centre of the labyrinth, he stops,
hearing what you can hear
from where you stand: his own footsteps.

~

The place, the props, the ploys.
Debauchery, discovery,
deceit, damnation, death . . . of *course* it plays.

~

Not now, not yet, but maybe when we're older:
a cake-walk out to the harbour bridge,
a slow waltz on the hard-shoulder.

Spatchcock

As I entered, she had her pinking shears to the backbone,
having dropped the gizzard into the kitchen bin,
and barely looked over her shoulder to see who it was

when I gave the door a little back-heel
then ferreted round in the fridge for an ice-cold Coors
before slipping up from behind to cop a feel.

Another hot day in September, and that the cause
of her half-baked look, brought on
by lying bare-assed in the garden all afternoon,

a flush coming off her, the veins so close to the skin
I could trace the flow like sap, could tongue-up the ooze
of sweat at the nape of her neck: and this the real

taste of her, like nothing before, like nothing I ever knew.
You have to go hard at it, either side of the spine,
all the time bearing down against the sinew,

then lift the long bone entire and get both hands
into the cut, knuckle to knuckle, and draw
the carcass apart, and press, till you hear the breastbone crack.

Looked at like that it's roadkill, flat on its back,
sprung ribcage, legs akimbo, red side up, and sends
a message (you might guess) about life lived in the raw.

So then it's a matter of taste: herb-butter under the slack
of the breast, perhaps, or a tart marinade,
to flatter and blend, spread thinly and rubbed well in.

She favoured the latter – that and a saltire of thin
skewers driven aslant from thigh to neck,
which might, indeed, have said something about her mood.

That done, she stripped off, gathering the oils and the balm
she'd need for however long the thing would take,
and went back to her place in the sun. It did no harm,

I suppose, to watch from an upstairs window: a hawk's-
eye-view as she lay there timing the turn
(face-up till you tingle, then flip) to brown but not to burn.

The marks of the griddle, the saltire, the subtle flux . . .
We ate it with lima beans and picked the bones,
after which we took to bed a bottle of bright Sancerre

and I held her down as I'd held her down before,
working her hot-spots with a certain caution and care
as she told me not here . . . or here . . . but there . . . and *there.*

I left her flat on her back and shedding a glow,
or so I like to think, as I slipped downstairs
and lifted, from a peg-board beside the hob,

her mother's (or grandmother's) longhand note on how
to spatchcock a chicken, or guinea, or quail, or squab,
or sparrow, even, with emphasis on that 'crack';

and lifted, as well, before I lifted the latch,
myrtle, borage, dill, marjoram, tarragon, sumac,
all named and tagged in a customized cardboard box.

Bloodvein

i.m.

Soft on a leaf, last of the garden exotica, found only at dusk and pale
as the face in the sick-bed except for that long line
going wing-tip to wing-tip, heartstring, nerve-track, a thread you might pull

were it not for the way she turns and settles her head, the long vein
in her throat showing lilac by lamplight. The shadows that peel
from her fingers as they spread must be part of some long scene

of doubt and decay where all of this plays out: the fractured pearl
of the creature's eye, the journey from leaf to lamp that has long been
written in, like your word to her, like hers to you as she palms the bitter pill.

Abstracts

To put it more plainly: the subject or design is what the artist intends in the picture. And his intention in a painting has a point of view to which his subject matter, that is the elements of the painting, will contribute as an integral part of the whole. The subject or design of the painting is, therefore, the painting itself, and all of the statements which it makes simultaneously.

MARK ROTHKO, 'The Artist's Reality'

Red

The skim on the surface of your soup, or the cut on your plate
in the Café des Anges, juices swamping the willow-pattern skiff
as she dabs her mouth with her napkin, your blind, blind date,

leaving a smudge, lipstick-and-gore, though there's still a worm
of gristle in the gap between her teeth.
Mood music, candlelight, wine, low voices in a world of harm,

the creature brought down, hindquarters heavy, hindlegs
broken by the dogs, its head held up, eyes wide,
the tangle and drag as a gralloch-knife unpegs

the bulk, all slippage and seepage, and the way she thumbs
a morsel into your mouth, or smiles your smile
back at you, lets you know that everything's just as it seems,

then back at the small hotel, she strips off quicker than you
might have hoped, pink as a new-skinned cat, all too
eager to have you by heart. Her cry tells you nothing new.

Purple

Surely, what first comes to mind is *purpill and pall*.
No? So is it what she is said to have said that night
when she breathed a secret and put the whole room on stall?

Not that? Then it must have something to do with the way,
in the fairytale when the twins are lost in the wood,
daylight suddenly deepens and it's run or stay or pray.

Still wrong? Rain in the hanging gardens then? That bruise
you can't account for? The colour of money, win or lose?
A Balkan liqueur that hits you where – Ah, yes, of course; the bruise.

Black

You know the room, or think you do, half-dark
and windowless it seems, though maybe
the shutters are dropped against the day, loose talk

from women in veils and something like a pulse
on the air when he opens the door and slips straight in.
The Loden coat, the old slouch hat, the hare-lip, so who else

could it be, right on time and keen to help? Think back
to those promises, all of them straight from the heart,
never asked for, never kept. The skin-trade . . . there's a knack.

It's been a lifetime coming but now you understand,
or think you do, why what you wanted wasn't what you planned.
They bring a tray to your bedside. You eat from his hand.

Blue

It sings they say, and so it does: something like the note
that fractures glass or gets so far below
the range of human hearing that it shakes your heart;

and the glass it breaks is blue, and that's a blue note for sure
from the guy on the alto sax in the basement dive,
which is where they're bound to meet up in the classic *noir*,

the private eye, the girl with a shadowy past, the old-style cop,
and it's nigh-on certain she'll have to take a bullet
or we'll see her in prison blue as they lead her to the drop.

The fragments of glass were part of it too, that's plain,
though no one noticed, just as they failed to spot
how the crucifix in her bedroom made sense of the subtle stain

on her cocktail dress. And in this, the director's cut,
the dive is deeper, the saxophone sadder, the cop
bent as a dog's hind leg, the girl a scheming slut,

and the gumshoe comes in late with the one and only clue
that would finally set things straight, though its true
meaning is hidden from him, and lost on you.

Green

That misericord with the ugly little fucker
at the moment in his dance when slap-and-tickle
has become a serious matter, and no one's quicker

in getting his hand up the skirt of some 'ladie fayre',
who returns to hearth and home with the rub of the green
on her back for all to see and devil-may-care,

his smell still on her, reek of the barley mow,
and hers on him, which could have been sloe
or sweat and sandalwood, but you'd be the one to know.

Contre-jour

Dark-blue of dawn, deserted streets,
a light fall of soot in the rain, a man out alone, the faint

asdic of his footfalls off the pavement, the city
stirring round him, rumble of engines underground

or what might be a furnace starting up . . . A dawn
like any other, a nowhere city, the man myself.

⌒

I could tell I was cold, I could tell I was lost, I could feel
the grit from a sleepless night under my eyelids

and that slow, sour churn in the gut
of cheapjack wine. Morning shadows rolled

low along gutters and sills, like ground-mist shrouding
the gods of the black back-alleys, gods of the threshold.

⌒

I remembered a half-remembered dream of falling,
the sky on fire, cloud-wrack a bled bruise, wingbeats

drumming the wind. Blind and breathless. Numb
to my fingertips. I spread my arms and howled and trod plain air.

My descent was a kind of dance. The shadow shifted.
When I came to the cross-street I knew which way to go.

⌒

The underpass stank of sleepers. Trucks overhead
had opened a web of fault-lines that carried a dark dew:

enough to root pale, pin-head flowers. A man got up
from his mess of bedding, then, and kept pace with me,

unspeaking, his eyes on the light ahead, but he reached
out and picked me a flower: it brightened as the stem snapped.

~

He walked me as far as the river and left me there.
The cloud broke. Sunlight surged on the water and ran to black

by factory footings. A bell began. I seemed to see him again
clean-cutting the surface, feet first from the bridge,

past hulls and anchor chains . . . and days of drifting
before he snagged, wide-eyed, on the river's sunken iron.

~

By wharves and warehouses; gulls on the garbage scow;
the graffiti was all about love and remedies for love.

Stone steps took me into the backstreets; there came a cry
of pleasure or pain from an open window, and something in that

I seemed to recognise: not the voice, not the place,
but the way she broke off as if it might come to laughter.

~

The city square at midday, raked by light from a cloud.
A skinny dog went through, bone cranking bone.

A café on one side; on the other, a church . . .
And suppose I might have been content with that,

a splash of neon, the rose window, unanswered silence . . .
Suppose I might have found a way to sit and wait.

~

The memory's long since lost, but still there's a sense
of someone at my shoulder, of someone beyond the door,

of a voice somehow trapped in the room, although the words
are shuffled and split; or there's something barely held,

a photograph gone grey, as if dusk had blotted everything
except for a shape out of shadow turning towards the night.

~

The city as stone and steel, as silt and litter. Those moments
when the roar from the grid holds off, a dynamo winding down,

and the sorrowing call to each other through the birdsong.
I got to the edge and turned. The backdrop sky was white;

for just that moment, everything stood in negative:
the whole place mapped onto itself; the city as guesswork . . .

~

Petrol haze on the bypass. Wayside shrines
of the accident black-spots, votives catching the wind.

I'd been on the road a while before I felt
a sense of loss, or was it need of forgiveness? Even now

there are times when I wonder if that was the least of it:
the bridge, her cry, a flower drawn from darkness.

Suburb

What he heard was not an axe-stroke,
though the thin ring of it sang in his ear for a day.

What she heard was not water over stone
though its endless sameness ran her ragged.

Their house bred deep silences, broken sometimes
by the clack and clatter from some unreachable room.

First frost, the onset of evening, the expected guest.
What she hears now is neither man nor beast.

The Queen Bee Canticles

for Christopher Penfold

The Queen and the Philosopher

Sun on the sea running white, sun on white walls, yes, on the thick
shoulders of the fishermen as they fanned their nets, sun

as an engine, a trapdoor, a compass, Democritus in his cell
the window framing sea and sky, blue climbing on blue, a glaze

shaken by the heat, as she drifted in and held heavy
in the thickening air. It was this: a man writing,

herself as witness, the swarm now stalled and gorged.
When I die, bury me in honey. Fill an amphora

*three times my height, five times my bulk, then let me down
into it gently, a long soft glide . . .* His hand shook at that,

feeling himself poised in the moment, mouth filling,
eyes drawn blindly open, his penis stirring and settling.

Noon in the sculpture garden. They hung, with the lightest of touches,
from the outstretched marble arm of the goddess Athena.

The Apiarist Dreams of the Queen

When he picked her up in the Palais de Danse she was wearing
her downtown dress: soft stripes; behind her dark glasses, her eyes

were darker still. The floor was theirs. They did the jitterbug,
they did the Electric Glide and, oh, she was light to the touch.

The glitterball slowed and stopped. He followed her out
to a part of town where the sights and sounds didn't marry

and shadows fell slack in the streets. She had a room
in a white clapboard apartment-block and there they stayed

for a week or more (but this was dream-time, remember,
when things come fast and smudged). There was low-pitched music

on a loop-tape and snaps of herself, in that self-same dress,
with dancing partners who had about them a feverish look, a touch

of delirium: just what he felt each time she drew him in. He turned
in his sleep. Her breasts were honeycombs and her womb a hive.

The Queen in Rapture

A summer of storms. A stone-built Norman church. Hives in the graveyard.
The priest an incomer who preached only sin and redemption.

There you have it. Oh, and on one of the corbels
a bee in flight, flanked by a jack-in-the-green and a manticore.

They swarmed in heavy weather, low-slung and singing.
Light touched the apostles window as they found their way

down the transept and past the rood screen, then rose to the crucifix
taking hold on the Man of Sorrows, his tallow flesh,

until the priest knocked them off with a yard-broom,
so they dropped, howling, onto his head: from neck to scalp

a spinning ball of bees however he turned, however he beat at them.
And the queen in the midst, her frantic dance

in perfect time with his, so thrilled by his passion she stung
his lips, his tongue, his eardrums, his eyelids, his eyeballs.

The Egyptian Queen

On the fourteenth day, as they broke the door to the chamber, there came
a soft gonging from somewhere deep; the ground beneath their feet

rippled, enough to coat their boots with dust. And, touch by touch,
    the light . . .
Canopic jars, grave dolls, small flasks that once held honey. The
    catafalque

cracked under their hands; and, when they shifted the lid, a cloud of bees
came out, although . . . *came forth* . . . was what she wrote, the only woman

to see this: unmarried, a known hysteric, soon sent home to 'rest
and repair', her journal somehow lost. The gateway stela gave clues:

I FED TO THE WOLVES SMALL CATTLE . . . [lacuna] . . . CLEANSE ME . . .
[lacuna] . . . TEARS OF RA . . . The locals knocked up a basic counter-
    weight gantry,

then worked through the night by Tilley-lamp to crate
the smaller stuff, before chiselling the image of Anubis off the frieze.

The flasks were etched with a hieroglyph depicting a bee,
which does mean 'bee' . . . *came forth the queen, dark-eyed and tremulous.*

The Queen Redivivus

The Queen of Heaven stooped on by the angel: queen of the hive
attendant, her true token. As the risen Christ ate honeycomb, they say.

⌇

Sun through soft rain; the salt smell of blood; the fallen whitening to bone.
She found the eye-slit of a Viking helmet: sweetness in the field of death.

⌇

Cranach's more-than-naked Venus, her come-hither look, Cupid swatting
at the queen and her entourage: *Private Collection (Adolf Hitler; Munich)*.

⌇

Cornish tinners at Blackheath. Bees in the heather. The leaders taken
    and drawn
at Tyburn, where she made her nuptial flight, her paramours likewise
    disembowelled.

⌇

An exemplum – so thought Marx – for their zeal and polity.
She could hear the virgins piping. She broke out. She killed them all.

⌇

Joseph Beuys as shaman, his head anointed with honey and gold leaf,
in his arms a dead hare. He glosses, then, The Queen Sculpted from Beeswax.

⌇

A hammock between two apple trees, and just a touch light of midday
when I felt her presence. The toxin blossomed under my skin, red-ripe.

Three Poems After Cavafy

Afternoon Sun

They are renting out the room, this room
and the room next to it, the room
I know so well, they are renting every room
in the house, a house of rooms
rented to agents, to clerks, to businessmen.

A sofa stood by the door, a Turkish carpet
in front of the sofa; on that shelf,
two yellow vases, yes, and off to the right,
– or was it? – a wardrobe, its fly-flecked mirror,
then the table, a pen, a half-done poem,
three wicker armchairs, yes,
and beside the window, our bed.

(Somewhere, that old stuff
must still be knocking about.)

Beside the window, our bed. Yes.
The afternoon sun
crept over it as we lay there: over us.

At four o'clock on one such afternoon
we parted
for just a week . . . a week or so . . . forever.

At the Tobacconist's Window

A small crowd at the neon-lit window
and these two, these among many . . .
Their eyes, as if meant to, snag softly,
something of sex there already,
then they walk off, although maybe
unsure until one smiles discreetly
and catches a nod – only barely.

They drive, they park up . . . They are so
careful about how best to go
here and go there, lips and hands going slow
as they fall on each other, but gently.

The Art of Poetry

They get out of bed. They get dressed.
They don't speak a word. Then they split,
both of them seeming a touch
shaky, now, as they leave
(not together, of course) and hit
the street. It's easy to guess
from each wide-eyed look as they pass
that enough was just too much to give.

Nothing unusual in this,
but the poet has just caught a whiff
of a song coming on (maybe soon,
maybe not) that will start with the line
They get out of bed. They get dressed . . .

Night

Insomnia: that great educator.
CORNEIL LEFEVRE

I

This can only occur at night; it's how and why he's woken
to stillness, wide-eyed, in a frowzy nest

of broken images the best of which inflicts
a rich reward on that faithless bitch he'd more than half-forgotten.

His bone-breaker laugh
unlocks the doors, starts the pump, brings on the boiler, lights the lamp,

uncaps the single malt. Maybe she'll star
in *Sluts I'd love to hump* or *MILF gets ripped*, a tell-tale stain

curdling the white of her eye. We'll see. A gentle rain sets down
on the skylight. At this dead hour it must be right

to celebrate the serial sots, the virtuoso piss-
artists, who drink to wipe the slate, to leave no trace. He tops his glass

and salutes their grace-in-misery no less
than the naked rage, the face-off with fate, the shaken cage, the loss

of hearth and home, of a room much like the one
he sits in now, forfeit to a slip of the tongue, to the last

and best of the bottle, the hot synaptic blip
that somehow bridged Friday and Monday, the taste of heavy metal

in gutter-waste. A black breeze stirs the rainfall;
the window gives onto darkness and that's all. He's blind to chance

and he knows it. The lost girl and the drunks
are regulars in the nightly song-and-dance, the real-time dreams.

Is it wrong to be so addicted to grime and grief?
Perhaps; but he'll see this out: sidelined, in hock to happenstance.

II

The gulp and lurch of apnoea, a full five-second blank,
no help for it; he tanks then breaks the surface with a yelp,

his body out of place, as if he'd torn
and repaired cockeyed, himself reborn, which must be why he hears

the voice instructing him on how to better live his life, to give
more than is received, to recompense the deceived, to make amends

for all that's yet to come, to muck-out the slum he calls a mind,
to sign away his nest-egg of regret, to scrub the list of sorrows, to forget

the twist in the tail, the badass schemes, to swim
no longer in the river of dreams, to finally drop his fist,

to accept that everything is more or less what it seems:
whisky-fever, birdsong out of darkness.

III

A quarter moon, livid like a burn-scar. An airbus drops
into the Heathrow corridor. A vixen yips with pleasure-pain.

Time to backtrack, time to review his bond
with calamity, the usual brand of folly, the necessary payback

to the dark-eyed tallyman. A radio voice
updates him on the party at the end of the world: his plan

for which involves the girl of his dreams, his drug of choice
and to stand four-square to the meteor as it streams

through the troposphere trailing
clouds of glory, seas boiling, the air on fire

and the earth singing deep in its core . . . The voice gives way
to radio silence; a step on the stair

reminds him: a room in a sunlit square, the girl
in question, the rule they made always to ride their luck

which left them, soon enough, looking back and looking up
at the room from the street, having shed the names

they knew each other by, hearing the last, lost beat
of the music that, one time, drew them in, and nothing clear

or certain ever again: the slow shifting of woodland at dusk;
a border crossing, unmapped; the unwalkable roofscape silhouette.

IV

From the window, lights of windows and the brittle, thin
example of himself almost within reach, almost shoulder to shoulder

with what might seem the real thing
somewhat older and closer to the dark, the image broken

by bars of shadow, a strikeout, the back-reflected racks
of stuff he'll never read or listen to. His night-long stakeout

brings a sudden wonderment, a small procession
of ghosts among fern and dogwood before they turn their backs

and drift down the garden path, as if the dead
really had somewhere to get to, as if the life-long burden

of things unsaid might be dumped in such a place,
or a blood-debt settled, or a curse unravelled thread by thread.

Their own weather comes with them, a sort of smothering,
then owl and night-crow together, home to roost.

Nothing as hard as memory lost-and-found, nothing as sad
as these refugees of the false dawn. From the window, a graveyard.

v

Here is the news. Whatever you most despise will have its day;
money will rise from the dead; expect to see

strangers lining the streets; reports now indicate
the saving grace will surely come too late; a wall of rain

and sheet lightning like flak the weathermen advise:
the long reach of Abu Ghraib feedback, of IED kickback.

Watching this unfold, himself and no other; the skies
fill then fade to black. 'He was my sole delight,' says the grieving mother.

VI

A loose door knocking in an empty house;
a mirror framing a single reflection, undisturbed; a chair

still somehow bearing the weight . . . He's dreamed all this before
and seems to wake in that unearthly place

sanctuary of the weevil and the louse,
slippage behind the skim . . . except he's rough-hauled back

on a stalled breath to the night-watch
that substitutes for the dream; his duty then to check

statistics, to itemise the download, to keep track
of the trade in flesh, of the how and where and when of the recent dead,

of traffic in the city of ashes, city of lies and loss,
of the breakage and spillage, the more-is-less, to take especial note

of the burnouts, the turncoats, the hard cash used to freight
the pockets of the drowned man, of the life-in-light

promised to all who gave their names,
of the way the whole grid dims when someone throws the switch,

of the perfect match power makes with innocence, of games
played out to the last man in the last ditch, of the mendicant poor

in seemly rows, the wayside shrines, the cry
that returns and returns, the empty houses, the men awake at windows.

VII

A troubled mind. Black actuality. The little wheels
that tick and turn. How it feels when the mad machine cranks up

and the room breeds shadows out of dusk. The small, bright burn
of recollection. The way each image feeds

off the last, and so proceed. The unborn,
as if they knew. Debt and reckoning. The sudden jostle and press

of faces in the glass. The smell of lechery. The one sure thing,
unchanging, unable to change. The last of the safe places.

The long, low tremor of grief. The chain of dreams. The loss
that might have gone unnoticed except –

The night-wind again. The shape of a slow dance in air: the way
she would enter a room bringing nothing with her

or what passed for nothing. A state of shame.
How blame goes from hand to hand, a truth best told

in the fable of the leper's kiss. How the dead come home, as they must.
How nothing repairs or restores. How love will enable fear.

The way words dissolve in air, even the best.
The depth of darkness. The heartbeat rhythms of prayer.

VIII

That time backs up in a stopped clock is the only way to explain
how every night is one night, topped and tailed

by the same ill-wish, same terror, same storyboard
in which his anger kindles a dirty flame; and still

the same chair, same book, same page: *In plain air then I fled,*
but the Godhead stalked and stunned me; there I fell,

on my knees among the furrows, lost and found . . .
And the self-same radio voice with the worst news, as before;

and the girl in the two-minute movie, her raw pink;
and the first drink calling on the next; and the double deal

of the self-told lie; and sleep-in-waiting as a nest of rooms
in the smallest and deepest of which a narrow bed

summons its dreamer . . . yes, and his face looking back
from the window wherein he seems to cry and seems to speak.

IX

In this, the Bridge of Sighs; in this, pi-dogs
scavenge a tip; in this, the soft disguise of kohl and candlelight;

in this, his heavy smile; in this, a bright
gunmetal gleam where sea and sky collide; in this, they're laughing

at a child in tears; in this, a novice bride
takes to the floor; in this, the last of its kind stares through the bars;

in this, a water-garden beyond an open door; in this,
a woman walks through naked . . . There should be some kind of law

to govern such vigils: the images flow in and flood; the clock
fights back; his heart holds off a moment. In this, the city's all-night
   glow.

   x
He dreams his room as a breeze-block lock-up, place of pain,
wall of manacles, blindfold and gag, a thing in freeze-frame

that won't come into focus, but seems to sag
into its own blurred weight, blotched where you might expect

to find eyes or mouth, blotched where it breaks or forks.
The keyholes are plugged, the doors blindsided, a cross-hatched spread

of light rolls out across the concrete floor, as if a streetlamp shone
through a window-grille; this is a dream where the sun

never quite comes up, where he goes in dread
of clean skins on the airbus, a knock from the coffin, the dead end

doubling as the sheer drop, where he finds himself a full step light
of the room at last; and there's nothing, now, to hold the man
   from the night.

Necrophilia

No wayward promise, nothing to shake the heart,
nothing to warm to, no trace of harm or hurt,

nothing of jealousy, no risk of bliss,
the wide, white eye; the perfect parting kiss.

Elsewhere

First of the night and this ae night it's gin,
straight up with a twist, a chunky shot-
glass to the brim and down in one
as if there were a gun
to my head, though one's soon gone
and never enough, my gillyflower,
to stall the hour or likewise stop the rot.

Blissful to roam the house amid the spoor,
the allergens, spindrift we shed
and breathe, our little muckhill, dander of the dead.
Blue light of the inmost hour.
Shadows in corners are doing what shadows should.
Our curtains are winding sheets,
our rugs the grave-cloths of the Godless poor.

The landing just outside the bedroom door,
is where the spook from last night's dreamscape meets
the Demon of the Stair: I brush them off
and sashay down a flight, then one flight more
and then, somehow, a third, as if some rough
logic could make the kitchen floor my roof
and draw me through a cobwebbed corridor

that opens to a grid of empty streets,
where you and I must go, my love, my jilliver
(if, indeed, it's really her
shadowing me: that 'light-heeled dame', that 'wanton in the last
stage of her good looks'. Except . . . who else, who else?)
One turning, then another, and I'm lost.
There's music from somewhere, perfectly timed to my pulse.

A cellar bar. And someone guessed that mine's a marguerita
the nip of salt on my lip, the bite of lime,
nothing remarkable in that, except I have to wonder
how you got here in so short a time
(but the table-lights are dim, and when I cross to greet her
she's taller and darker and older and speaks with a candour
that scorches my cheek). Things are not what they seem

is as far as I've got with this: the barman pouring
one for the road that takes all night to hit the glass,
neon staining my breath, reflections in the mirror tearing
like tissues and that barfly with the blue-black gloss
to his quiff who beckons me over and pats the stool
next to his, as if he'd been keeping my place
for half a lifetime, and smiles at me as a joker smiles at a fool.

'I never envied another man's life,'
he says, 'the way I've envied yours, the full and fine
day-after-day of it, a house so full of song, a wife
so sleek and quick to please, your music, your books,
those times in the summerhouse with friends and wine;
or candles shifting the shadows, and soft rain
stippling the darkened window as she turned to you again.

'But more than anything, I envy this: the day you woke
to the knowledge that true sacrifice is gain
and junked the lot, setting out at once, a bleak
road ahead of you, the weather closing in, her last
desperate kiss still cooling on your cheek;
and I'm more jealous of that touch than of the least
part of what you'd just flushed down the pan.'

The music is soupy blues, she in her patchy satin
working her way through the clientele – a dance
for a double-and-chaser, with (I guess) a pretty fair chance
of better later – and this booze-blind cretin
confusing me with someone he once met in
another bar another time, so I'm just getting set to coast
towards the door I came in by, as her glance

slaps the back of my head and when I turn
we're standing nose-to-nose
and hip-to-hip, the curve of her lip, the slow burn
as she lifts her eyes to mine, and dips, and flows
out onto the floor, myself in tow, her civet-and-myrrh
drawing me on, 'Fine and Mellow' on the turntable, her mouth
close to my ear as she whispers, 'There's a dearth

of men like you and that's the truth.
Tell me again about the day you turned your back
on everything dear and took the stony track
that led away from your house and hearth – the death
of the old without sight of the new. Tell me again
how you wrung her tears from your shirt, how her pain
was the little light you carried to find your path

after nightfall, and how her few last words
became the first line of the song you sang to keep
your spirits high as you traipsed the starless black.'
I try to pull away, but she holds me hard
grazing my cheek with a kiss as she dances me back
to the door. A cheery wave from the creep
at the bar and I'm out on the street, in weird weather,

the sky a lemon-yellow shot with red, and silent birds
climbing the wind. On the corner
a skinny brindled dog is looking over its shoulder,
then, as I get close, cranks itself into a bony G,
drops a little pile of thin, black turds,
and trots ahead as if I were its owner.
The fleabag leads, I follow, through a tumbled scree

of bottles and cola cans and KFC,
which puts me in mind of the time we climbed a tor
in weather that kept a dozen crows aloft
like smuts in an updraft, the sea on one side, dimmed
by rain, on the other side the moor,
and sat backed up to the blow, our faces crammed
together in kisses at the same time hot and deft,

she with her, 'Nothing to hide,' me with my winning smile
and stone-cold certainties, the path we'd travelled by
snaking back to the point where it seemed to drop
right off the edge. That was a time of trial.
That was when we lived life on the fly:
nothing slow or solemn, nothing dark or deep.
Everything I got I got by guile; everything I had was mine to keep.

So it's no surprise that you find me walking blind
down an empty street, wading through wind-blown crap
and following this leggy, brindled hound:
clearly, I'm next in line for the sudden slap
in the face that a jealous future holds in store
for the cod-philosopher, the housewife-whore
and others who shape their lives with whatever falls to hand.

Rain coming up and streetlights coming on
and darkness coming in that just won't settle.
Natural light is urban twilight here –
orange in the undercloud, gunmetal
grey, a seepage of damson: heaven's wear and tear . . .
You know how you catch a whiff (and then it's gone)
of whatever it takes to take you back – or perhaps you hear

something that means nothing to anyone
but you? It might be a cheap pomade; it might be a sound
much like a goat, or else a child in pain –
just such a smell, in fact, and just such a sound, that leave me
with my nose to the window of this end-
of-terrace two up, two down
and peering into a room where kitsch is king, believe me,

from the chintz and plaster dogs to the cruet-set,
his Fair Isle jersey, her blouse and Crimplene slacks.
They bid me enter (yes, *bid*), suggesting that I sit
at the head of the table. The dog slopes past and cracks
a fart, then finds a corner and flops like any pet.
'Are you thirsty at all?' he asks. 'Are you hungry: is that it?'
She lays a laden plate before me and I flex

my fingers like a concert pianist.
'Plain food for a plain man,' she says. Now my intention
is to eat them out of house and home, to go hand over fist
at whatever they bring on.
She steers the hostess-trolley. 'Did I mention
your bed's made up, your stuff laid out, from first to last,
and neither him nor me counting the cost?'

Five minutes go by, or else five hours; either way, the trick
is to somehow get through the long, slow haul
from loving to leaving. 'Are you the long-lost or the prodigal,'
he wants to know, 'or maybe the one and only?
Look, wherever you've been, whatever you've done,
it's nothing to us. Eat yourself sick,
drink yourself daft, don't say a word, pretend you've just begun.'

A meal like that can put you on your back
but leave you wanting more: just like that summer night
of truth or dare when we took up the slack
at Harlequin, moved on to Jimmy Dean's, then took a cab
the whole way back, too wrecked to fuck or fight.
I woke next morning, a man laid on a slab.
You woke in another place, a woman on the rack.

All food's a sacrament.
Rain blurs the room. The sky shuts like a lid.
Shadows crowd the door. I know I should repent
everything known against me and everything I hid:
days of grand illusion, days of loss, gilded words that went
for nothing, smiles meant for no one, all the luck
falling to either the monstrous or the moonstruck.

The dog stands at the door. On the sofa, there, a perfect *primitif*
of Him 'n' Her moved beyond measure by grief,
watching me step by step as I cross the room;
but then he's on his feet and reaching for a book
that sits between Patience Strong and The Ten Minute Cook.
'Take this, it's yours.' He's right, of course, the flyleaf
carries my name in schoolboy minuscule, a bloom

of mildew on the boards, the pages foxed, the spine
broken, that indelible first line
shaking my heart: *I mind as if it were yesterday*
my first sight of the man. Little I knew at the time
how big the moment was with destiny . . .
Now, more than ever, it seems possible to cram
everything into the instant, to kiss them both, to say

that I've lived my life thinking the past a crime
when in truth it was nothing more than shadowplay.
Perhaps if I knew their names; or knew a way
to take with me only what's mine . . . Back on the street,
empty-handed, bare-headed, a wind
shifting the rain in bundles, a tiny torrent of grime
tumbling in the gutter, I go through it again and find

that nothing remains but their lardy smiles, their blind
faith, their hand-in-glove.
Between them, more than a lifetime spent in search
of another name for sorrow, another name for love,
nothing true as stated, nothing begun as planned,
but always the notion they might somehow catch
misery on the wing and turn it round.

There are shapes in the rain that I almost recognise,
warped by the downpour, reflections of reflections,
that become, as the silver curtain lifts and parts,
these shopfront mannequins, their anglepoise
wrists, their perfect breasts and lips and hair.
It's easy to see, from the way each coolly shuns
the others, that something once choice is now beyond repair.

Pale untouchables . . . not least the one who clambers down
to pavement-level, letting grey rain pearl
on her shoulders and run slick to the small of her back.
'You'll remember me,' she says, 'by a certain velvet gown
and tear-drop earrings to match a crystal-and-jet
choker, our window open, a cobbled square, a peal
of bells, the radio tuned (have you got there yet?)

to something sweet and low, music and mood
in harmony, nothing contrary, nothing unspoken, it seemed,
in a night that drifted soon enough from good
to bad, from bad to worse.' The shock
takes my breath away; this girl
standing before me naked and numb to the wet
is the very image of one last seen beside the track

on a railway station in outer suburbia, the slack
of her mouth, the tilt of her head, the folded arms,
more than enough to write the opening lines
of a novel in which the main man turns his back
and walks away, unspeaking. After a while, she leans
(or so he imagines) against the metal pole that holds the name
of the place and picks at flakes of rust. *But still a flame,*

the writer assures us, *burns behind her eye, though whether lit
by love or revenge not even she could tell.* And by the time
she boards the train, the man's well on his way
to 'Elsewhere', a location where problems soon surrender
to geography, and history corrupts.
To be brought up short this way in a downpour, and get hit
with a hard-edged slab of the distant past, would render

any man no less speechless than the bastard in the book,
especially when faced with her level look,
those cold, blind breasts, that slender
neck where a hand might usefully rest, the bald pudenda
sealed to sex for ever. She interrupts
whatever it was I almost said, and takes me back
to that room, the deepening dusk, the square, some madcap swifts

circling between the Palace of Delights and the rotunda:
'Why is it,' she asks, 'that memory never adapts
or softens or finds peace in forgiveness? – The wind shifts,
birdsong turns sour, the snapshot blurs and fades, another blunder
leaves us out on the edge, a cold night coming on,
some rawness on the skyline like a wound
puffing and purpling. Are you proud of yourself, I wonder,

having *just dropped everything*, having *turned
your back*, having *changed your life*, to be found
facing the way you're facing and thinking the way
you're thinking, the skyline silhouette, the stoic singleton,
(apart from that bony brindled bitch),
yourself taken up by the very swing of your arm, the pitch
of your stride, and no one to guess the why

and wherefore of the abandoned meal, the book
thrown down, the door left on the latch.
Do they come to you in dreams, the woebegone, and lie
to you as you lied to them?
Do they give you a glimpse of all that you forsook
then let it drift through their fingers? Do they sigh
for truth as once they sighed for the perilous and the sham?'

How come those sightless eyes can stare me down? How come
those seamless lips still make my own lips itch?
(The refugee's nostalgia for the slum,
the snake-charmer's sordid contract with the snake.)
'Listen,' I say, as I stoop to kiss her off,
'nothing is yea or nay or sink or swim or make or break.
Fucking leads to kissing, that's the catch.'

Back among her own she turns aside and sets her face
to its own reflection, chin lofted, thus,
fingers splayed, arms up and elbows out, the frozen grace
of a body in free fall, as those of the sisterhood
also shudder and stall, the streaming glass
casting onto their cheeks the like of bitter tears
that any man, you'd think, would surely plunder if he could.

The cobbled square, the swifts . . . And who is that
sitting alone in the half-dark room, half drunk,
the fading smudge of sundown on the wall
like a slipping tide, the fatal note
still unwritten while the last of *Heart Like A Wheel*
settles in corners and all the shadows shrink
to a single profile that holds its own against the coming night?

Such vigils have their own spillage and stain,
their own detritus, torn things, things cast aside,
things bartered without any hope of gain,
and someone – one of you – is put to seeing-in the dawn,
as if 'grey' were right for this, as if 'chill' were right,
then sitting on through the day, bottle to hand,
with nothing left to give, nothing to hide,

the best of what was squandered still in sight
and that life forfeit, sure, but everything else untried.
Solo and glad, though not at all as planned:
sleep comes soon enough, and dreams to place the dreamer
in a landscape of grasses and water, a heavy sky,
black cumulus dragging up from thin horizons
and distances to cheat the eye.

Stain on the leaf, a wind across the flats
salty and dry that would surely skin the cheek
of anyone stranded there, a figure frozen
by guilt, maybe, or else by indecision
unless that skinny dog returns, as to its own puke,
nipping and nudging, then a ground-mist that floods and floats
with corpse-lights to guide, the sort of dream-fluke

that changes everything, the scene, the weather,
the way you feel which, in my case, is A-OK
with the dog a step ahead, as always, its long nose sleek
to the air or, sometimes, glancing back across its shoulder
to check me out . . . and the sway
of its tucked-up rump raises in me a thought
that I can't quite hold, though it turns on the verb 'to tether',

which, itself, reminds me of something someone said
on the subject of freedoms given and freedoms taken
(just another piece of lumber in the head)
as we break from sedge-and-rillet to brier-and-whin,
then clifftop turf, then sight of the sea, a feather
of foam on the tips of the waves as they line up
to drop their payload of plastic and cans and nylon rope

on the darkening foreshore where, now, a beacon burns
that might, in a tale like this, be a wreckers' lantern,
or else be the last lost hope
of the lovelorn as his ship puts out in heavy weather,
the pall of her shadow dimpling on the stones,
that gathering flame their marker and their token,
watched and kept until the long blue drag of the horizon

is met in a moment when everything dissolves,
not least his promise, not least her gift of smiles,
and he turns his back to the land, unless it's she who turns
for home, brisk in the wind and *keening* no doubt;
but this fire, as it happens, soon resolves
to a driftwood blaze and a sad old sack
who hands me a bottle of something dark and sour

that hits your heart as it passes, and I'm glad of it
what with a chill off the sea, the sky near-black,
and a sudden wind lifting stingers of loose sand
as I lend a hand with the spit he's rigged,
low to the fire and carrying, end to end,
a row of little corpses, that I reckon might
be songbirds or mice, racked up like an abacus,

and done to a crisp, though they pull apart
sweetly, good meat, tender and hot and wet,
a mouthful or two, just that, and the tiny bones still soft.
'You can take a fair few of these,' he says, 'with a mist-net
or a morsel of something rich and tending to rot
laid in a wicker cage.' He coughs
and hoiks up an oyster of phlegm, aiming it straight

at the seat of the fire. 'Can you guess how I came to this?
It's easy. There was a time when I had the best
of everything: money, a quiet life, just the right
balance between love and laughter, the morning kiss,
each day like a painting on glass. You know the rest:
a chance, a quickening, a lie, no thought of harm,
and then the long game that plays, always, to lapse and loss.'

I start to get to my feet, but he takes me hard by the arm.
'You of all people . . .' His hand drops, but the wet
of his eye, reflecting a lick of flame,
red in the iris and deep there, holds me. 'You should know
how all sin is sin of circumstance and time, all sadness too,
the tale we invent for ourselves, the inescapable,
the fate we spin from ambition and desire, the no-way-back,

the terrible notion of living life to the full,
the slow advancement of days, all comfortless, all lost
to pleasure, the pain of that, the rack
of memory, slow music, lights coming on at dusk,
all lost, windows wide to the night-air, children's voices lost
to the sound of surf, to the sea's clean sweep,
myself, pitched up, you might think, from anywhere, addled, lost,

as if I'd come to from a night-long dream of risk
that stationed me on this beach, as if to sleep
were to dream of the place I must wake to, dream
only of that, the tideline rubble, the pull of the waves, the scar
salt leaves on stone, the long, bright line
where the rest of the world falls away – and you, since here you are,
sent to some purpose, I reckon, if things are what they seem.

So what can you tell me, friend, that I don't already know?
What might you hand me that I don't already have
and already have to share with the black-backs and the terns?
Something of loss, perhaps? Something given over to the flow
of water and wind, or pressed to less than nothing by the shove
and nudge of shingle, some glimpse, some gleam
of a half-forgotten life in the dredge of the undertow?

Look, this is my place-to-be, now, this is my scheme,
whatever's to hand, whatever comes my way, whatever spurns
whatever you might want even more than you want love
or forgiveness or guidance or recompense for harm.
I'm the old man of the sea if you like, the wanderer,
I can bring fish to a whistle, birds to a spinning coin,
I can set you down by this very fire and hold you fast

with the tale of the maiden and the loathly worm,
the house with no door, the gallant roped to the mast,
or the man who spoke his mind,
fastened his eyes on darkness, and hunkered down in a cage
of secrets, refusing even the consolations of music,
until everything there is of love and rage
fell away, leaving him pale and purified and blind.'

I'm ready to counter this with a longer and finer list
when there leaks in a sudden touch of the true magic:
a standing moon in a deepening cobalt sky, the sea gone white
as if water could run under frost,
the cry of a seabird lengthening on the wind,
and the moment steady, and the whole thing held in sight,
and barely a breath to be had between first and last

while I walk to the cave where, I guess, he spends the night
and lift from his cache of flotsam and folderols
a tide-turned pebble with a broad, bright stripe of quartz
that sits in the palm of my hand
just so, as I make my way past a jumble of nets and creels
to where the back wall shows a sudden flush of lights
which can't be the moon off the sea, though something tolls

like a bell-buoy to warn me off, at which my thoughts
fall to a pattern of candlelight and shadow
and voices under the night-wind, as if I might brave
a glimpse of that life I left, or seem to have left, as if
I stood just beyond reach – a waking dream
that draws me, now, to some deeper part of the cave
where a cut in the rock opens up to a path of sorts,

the path to a lane, the lane to a torch-lit meadow
and the bell is a voice and the beat of the sea is a drum
and the song is that wild lament
of love and loss that must be set to tear
the heart of any woman who wakes, let's say, to dumb
certainties, to shades of rain, an empty house, a bare
memory of the first fell word, the last impediment . . .

The drummer, the singer, and there among the dancers
(unless it's someone who owns that self-same grace,
that half-smile like a litmus of the soul)
the one and only – else why does she break the dance
and lead me off to this nest in bracken
to do what has to be done, while the drumming blurs
and that heartbreaker voice finds a note that could punch a hole

in the fabric of the universe . . . and her breath on my face
(supposing it's her) gives everything away: that what stirs
in me is not love but all that stayed unspoken
and went to the bad; that hope is held to ransom
by virtue; that darkness unquenched is our true endowment;
that promises freely offered are better taken by force;
that nothing can mend in dreams what scorn has broken.

Having slept all night in her arms (of course) I wake
to birdsong in mist, our sweet annulment
the kiss I can neither avoid nor return, that winsome
look away, the tip of her tongue emerging to seek and take
a tiny globe of dew from her lip. Intent
on saving this to memory, I somehow fail to catch
her parting word as she slips through a sudden break

in the mist, her naked back washed in that pearl-and-rose,
her footstep too light to measure –
yes – and there, again, is the one itch I can't scratch:
a morning much like this and, as you might expect, a breeze
nudging the curtains, the drone of a plane, a scent
I know but can't quite place, a sense of pleasure
gone to waste: a missed chance, a wrong turn, a poor match . . .

My found-life in dreams. My life as escapade.
My life as lived by the man I want to be: that welcome hint
of sourness in song, the sly perfection of the ready-made.
I close my eyes in hope, but the hound
chucks my chin with her snout before moving off to hunt
a copse halfway uphill, and I make the climb
for no good reason at all, only to find

what I take to be a city of the plain
spread out before me, its towers lapped in a petrol-blue
canopy of cadmium – a place that, in the main,
should be off the map for a man whose mind
is fixed on forgetfulness, whose purpose grew
from a gritty *Don't look back*. What is it, then,
that draws me down to the outskirts, that pushes me on

through alleys and backstreets (the dog in her element
opening bin-bags to nuzzle the rich black mash),
that takes me past car-lots and workshops, past greasy spoons,
past walk-up and rack-rent,
past casinos and clubs and shebeens, past Mr Moon's
Tattoo Shack, past day-for-night hotels, past cash-
on-the-nail, past rat-runs and bargain bazaars, arcades,

dives and dumps, cross-cuts, bootleg cabs,
the house of correction and the house of jades,
fast food portals, a patch of green, or what was once
green, its litter of cans and condoms and needles, past
the damaged, the derelict, the up-for-grabs,
past flea-pits and burn-outs, no entry, no refunds,
no-win-no-fee . . . and there, in the city square, the last

honest man, the very picture of a hermit dunce,
wearing the starry look
of someone both in his skin and out of bounds.
To his left a fountain, to his right the monument
raised to that stern-eyed hero who went by the book
to save the day, leading someone a merry dance,
his name a purple tag, his fearsome bas-relief

hard-caked in pigeon-shit. Beyond the square,
a high-rise slum; beyond the slum, a dense
five-mile backup on the overpass, a brief
asdic-stutter of sunlight cutting the blue-black haze.
The Fool is dancing a little dance of grief
to a tune no one can hear
and his tip-tap footstep tells me, 'Follow if you dare.'

Past junk shops, past the wax emporium . . .
The dog is jittery. She sniffs the air.
The hackles lift on her spine as we walk into a maze
of alleys that seem to have never seen the sun,
and somewhere a cry of pain, and somewhere the slam
of a door that will never open until the job is done,
and the Fool some steps ahead, his loopy smile of smiles

a beacon in the gloom, his dance a quickstep now,
leading me on, streets like a birdless wood,
a rich and heavy smell I can't define . . . There's barely room
for the dog, myself and this skipping simpleton
when we reach the bottleneck that leads to a no through road
with its shuttered shops and the beaten-up façade
of the Picture Drome, a redbrick slum sporting a new

lime-and-lilac neon sign to advertise a show
I reckon I might have seen before
That smell I couldn't place? It's blood and sorrow.
So time to leave, of course, but I've gone too deep
to ever get back without my guide, whose grin,
is shakier now, who coughs in what might be fear
or deference, as he stops and waves me in.

Blood as bond; sorrow that clings to sleep.
In the velvet plush of centre-stalls, the hound at my feet,
I watch from behind my hand as they run
the movie: a garden in rain, a house lamp-lit,
a glimpse through an upstairs window as she lets slip
her evening gown and turns to draw the blind,
her look of love now shaded by regret.

Fade to black . . . A time-lapse, then, to find
the rain has stopped, the skies have cleared, and someone
is walking across the lawn towards the orchard
his face turned to the stars, turned to the moon,
starlight and moonlight in among the trees,
the fruit, in that fragile glow, heavy and pale.
Blood as bond; passion as style; joy as a slippery slope . . .

We follow him as he steps through a lattice of hard
shadows cast by the branches, and soon
he's lost to us, along with his sorry tale
of riven dreams and waste and abandoned hope,
which tale, as we know, isn't his alone
but is drawn from the Book of Books and goes like a wheel
to pitch up at your door some day in the shape

that always scared you most, that brings you face to face
with what you know to be the choice
of no choice, left hand/right hand, give or take,
whatever beguiled, whatever was set to break,
the stolen moment revealed, the outright lie
echoing down the decades; and the child
cries in her sleep and the weather grows slowly worse.

There's a soundtrack to this: music which seems to settle
like light on water, as if the curse
of love-in-solitude might scatter on the skim
and be swept away. She wakes to that same brittle
morning sunlight now, on what might be the next
day or week or month, depending on the scheme
or storyboard, depending on the whim

of whoever set this down, whoever fixed
the place, the moment, the move that brings her close
to camera, eyes wide, so you might well think a dream
still sheltered there, might think the image she casts
in her mirror could simply turn and walk away:
no word, no backward look, a print on glass, now dim,
now gone, to arrive a moment later on the brink

of that other life, the one she planned, the one
where nothing is lost to vanity or haste,
where sorrow translates to song
and the tug of the tide holds the world in place.
Though in fact what follows is montage and flashback, run
randomly, like a shuffled pack, and fast,
before anything else can sever, anything else go wrong,

no words between them, although we see them touch
as people do, sometimes, to test
the strength of what once held them, even when it's lost.
In one frame, she's reaching up, open-handed, the pose
of an *in memoriam* angel or shopfront mannequin;
in another, he's picking fruit in that self-same orchard; the rest
are day-to-day or by-the-by, but never face-to-face,

too much given over to gladness, too much given over to trust,
the slow loosening of hands, the sullen ruse,
night-music, a night-bird singing, the air growing thin,
then everything suddenly blurs and falls out of place,
images falter and lock, an unbreakable pause
that leaves them strung out between *backtrack* and *begin*,
sightless on the borders of the past.

Silence of slow water, silence of the rose
that burdened the summer, silence of the still unopened book.
Leave them with that. The dog's out cold, but snickers
and shows her teeth; meanwhile the Fool
is standing by the door where he snags me with a look
then hits the lights so there's only the neon flicker
of the exit sign to get me to the street

where I catch the last of him rounding a corner,
half-hidden by the mist that's pouring in
from God knows where, all sulphur and soot,
and myself, now, part of a shadow-play
in which old Billy Bones, a good deal leaner
than legend would have it, heaves up
out of the swim, and delivers the death-in-life salute

as he passes, that skinny hand colder and whiter than clay,
the white of his eye, the white on white of his grin, a sight
you'd hope never to see on such a day,
much less when the bastard's alter ego floats
into view, same nubby nose, same greasy teeth, a sweet
smell off him, like apple-rot, that hangs
in the thickening mist, only to be replaced

a moment later by a pungency no less rich and ripe
as another goes by, then another – seven in all,
as if the Old Man might now travel in gangs
each baldy, knock-kneed, club-faced ghoul a clone
of himself and each one eager to greet
someone like me: a man given just enough rope
to cut some slack or otherwise take the fall.

All things considered, my only hope
is to get in off the street somehow, before
fate comes round the corner hand in hand with chance,
each anxious to let me know it's time to reap
whatever it was I sowed, tares to the fire,
brands to the burning, the flame that purifies. A door
to my left stands open and I enter with scarcely a glance

at the magic square cut high on the lintel, or the elvin star
cast as a hologram there on the threshold, which now
claims my attention as it shimmies round my shoe
and draws me down a hallway draped in shadow
which leads to a triple arch, which leads (of course) to a stair
ascending to darkness. So on I go as if I had nothing to fear
though the stair is a cliff, though the dark is a hood,

and from somewhere comes a low whisper that could
be a warning voice, or could be my name
drifting down from an upper floor,
its broken syllables spoken with such weight
of sadness that something in me stalls, as if a dream
had picked up where it last left off . . . and there
she is in the guise of spaewife: the tiger's-eye ring, the jet

choker, the little velvet purse of black and white
pebbles that roll out the best and worst of what's to come.
Her room, as you might expect, is candle-lit,
a trace of smoke on crystal, a blade, a bird in flight
under glass . . . and set ready on the table, my natal chart
its mad cross-hatch of angles, its glyphs and gyres,
the *imum coeli* given as a cave or coomb

and nothing to say what lies beneath or beyond, nothing to say
whether that red-on-black is distant fires,
or the underglow of Hades, or just a slip of the hand.
How perfect, though, that her silks and satins float
in the buttery light as she settles with a sigh
to draw my future down; how perfect this double blind
where nothing predicted can ever go as planned,

where the rule of thumb is not 'you reap what you sow',
but how go the signs, how stand the stars,
what mysteries abide, what time or tide will find
the least and best of you; so when she stares
at a certain page of the chart and clicks her tongue, I know
that something is misaligned, something's broken-backed,
and my shadow-sign is waving from the wings.

'Look at the way,' she says, 'these lines are crossed and snagged
and the planets bunched like a fist; if everything's
as it should be, something's wrong: the odds are stacked
against you, and have been since the moment when you blagged
your way into her life, yourself as makeweight,
as the needful, the little bolt from the blue, only to ditch
the whole caboodle, complaining that too much freight

would sink you: too much hope-in-the-heart, too much
cap-in-hand, too much salt-in-the-wound, too much side-
by-side, too many dreams in monochrome, too high a risk
of waking wide-eyed to find the peaceable kingdom installed
in your own backyard.' My heart-line starts to itch,
which I take as a sign to give women like this a wide
berth in future. 'Your future,' she tells me next, 'is signed and sealed,

yes, cut and dried, unless – ' And she leans in close so the musk
of her perfume stings my throat, and speaks a word
I'd hoped not to hear . . . whereupon there breaks a pause so deep
and so profound it might have trapped starlight
or the tonnage of water at the top of the seventh wave,
and herself, it seems, caught up in that sudden sleep,
eyes wide, the word still on her lip, which makes this the right

moment to find the back way out: the stairs, a narrow slope
down to a door that opens on a path that leads to a garden gate
that lets on to a field of gravestones; and, though it's dusk
here if nowhere else, I can make out the inscription on the nearest:
Safe in the arms . . . as the dog squats to piss a yellow streak
on the granite marker done like an open book,
then trots off into the murk, whereupon I'm struck by the weirdest

sensation of being observed, my dazzler, my dearest,
by someone who knows what's next: someone who's kept pace,
kept watch *(I think of the spaewife's musk, the civet-
and-myrrh of the girl in the bar)* and something tells me it's best
to push on across the boneyard's clod and divot,
the sunken stones, the terrible scentless flowers: a place
given over wholly to sorrow, nothing ever forgiven, nothing at rest,

and the twilight a constant, thick enough to settle and drift
against these broken pillars and bare-faced angels.
The dog sniffs out some spoilage, which might be all that's left
of the dear departed, might be last night's tandoori, then slips
into some sort of fancy tomb or mausoleum, the outer door
jemmied, it seems, and standing open at one of the nine true angles
of darkness, and up from the deep a sound a lot like bells

which is, I discover, nothing more than the syncopated drip
of groundwater, nothing more than a death-dew, nothing more
than the way it rings on the ribs and on the skulls
of the long-since dead who line the walls,
roped off, upright, and dressed in what they wore
when they first arrived with a bloom in their cheeks, grave-dolls
stitched to a sleeve and a poke of silver coin

to buy their way out of hell, most with an eye on each other,
but one with an eye on me, or so it seems from the tilt
of the leathery head and the hollow stare
that is somehow burdened with notions of blame or guilt.
The dog's hunkered down at work on a collar-bone,
but it's time to make tracks so I give her a gentle kick
when a voice comes directly at me from the rack of hulks and hulls

which, of course, is only a wind leaking in, or is just
that skeletal hydraulophone, and the rest
heard only from within: 'My friend, it's plain to everyone
that your destination, *Elsewhere*, won't be found on any map,
and despite everything your journey was no true test
since the road that took you away is the self-same road
that has brought you round again, all that you loved now lost,

all that you fear still marking your footsteps' – a fall of dust
shakes from his gappy grin – 'and whether you count it mishap
or folly, whether you still think it possible to raid
the sublime, or absolve yourself from memory, or offload
your share of everything tainted or flawed,
it's nonetheless a fact that you're faced with a simple choice
which is, as I think you know, go on or go bust.'

The echo rings into the dark . . . it rings inside my head,
and it's not so much that he points or gives me the nod,
more that the whole bony row seems to stir and shudder, as if
something trembled beneath, some tiny seismic shift
going from one to the next and travelling deeper down,
which gesture I follow into the tunnel beyond, into the blackout,
which is more than absence of light, is interstellar rift,

is the deep reach of dream-space, wherever those dusty stiffs
have spent the last hundred years: the whispers, the weeping, the clog-
and-jostle of frail invisibles, until a scrap of light,
a tortured rhombus, much like Holbein's famous anamorph,
cuts through it, which I guess to be the rag-
end of someone's dream (not mine) with its insoluble ifs
and buts, the surrenders and reversals, the tears-by-rote.

Moment by moment the image resolves to a bright
movietone clip of the house I put behind me whenever that was,
the mossy, underground corridor that took me out to the street,
above which is the kitchen, of course, above
which is the bedroom, and there you are *(who else, who else?)*
in your oyster satin gown, up at the window as ever, hand-in-glove
with yourself, and the dream, like you, captured in the glass:

a frame of the orchard, a frame of the summerhouse, a frame
in which something almost happens twice, that farce
of love and forgetting. See how the falling rain
is stilled a foot or so from the roof, how the upshot of the game
laid out in the shuttered room depends on dice
that are thrown but not yet landed, how the stain
hints at the white perfection of the sheet but fails to form.

So naturally my step falls short of the door, my hand
just short of the handle; then, in that moment of poise, there breaks
against the windows and walls a sudden wash
of music, *lachrimae*, heartache, the unstoppable bloodrush
that ought to draw me in, except now I stand
several paces further back than a moment ago; and it seems
that anguished chord drawn from a touchless past is all it takes

to set me out on the road, the dog at heel,
no thought beyond the next step, never mind the hush
in the air that signifies bad weather, a razor-slash
skyline, off-beat birdsong, the sun going down like a broken wheel;
and everything at my back, now, everything let slip
whatever the truth of it is, whatever will be kept from me in dreams:
that mournful music, her face in the glass, the sting of gin on my lip.